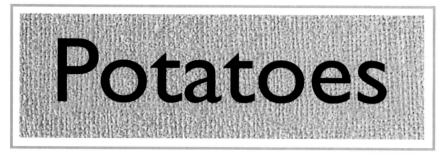

Potatoes

The Recipes

Asparagus & Potato Bake

4 medium-large potatoes

3 hard-cooked (boiled) eggs

1 x 8 oz (240 g) can asparagus spears, drained (liquid reserved)

1/4 cup (1 oz, 30 g) fresh, chopped dill

1/2 small chili, finely chopped

1 cup (2 oz, 60 g) grated cheddar cheese

1/2 teaspoon hot paprika

butter for greasing and browning

watercress for garnish

White Wine Sauce

2 tablespoons butter

3 cloves fresh garlic, chopped

2 tablespoons all-purpose (plain) flour

1 1/4 cups (10 fl oz, 315 ml) milk

reserved asparagus liquid

dry white wine to taste

1/2 teaspoon salt

juice of 1 lemon

Heat oven to 350°F (180°C, Gas Mark 4). Lightly grease a baking dish with butter. Peel, wash and slice potatoes. Boil until tender. Drain and quickly arrange half of them on the bottom of the baking dish.

Slice eggs and put them in a layer on top. Sprinkle with chopped dill and distribute the chili evenly. Spread most of the remaining potatoes out over the top again, reserving three even-sized slices.

Arrange the asparagus spears in a fan on top and then curve them around slightly. Arrange remaining potato slices on top before pouring over the sauce.

White Wine Sauce

Melt butter and sauté the chopped garlic until softened. Stir in the flour and cook until pale yellow. Remove from heat and add the milk, stirring quickly to remove lumps. Stir in the white wine to taste. Season and stir in lemon juice, stirring constantly. Return to heat and keep stirring, gradually adding in the asparagus liquid, until smooth and thick.

Pour sauce over the dish. Grate cheese over the top, sprinkle heavily with paprika and dot with butter. Bake for approximately 30 minutes until golden brown.

Serve hot, garnished with watercress.

Baked Potatoes with Stilton

4 large baking potatoes, approx 12 oz (375 g) each

2 tablespoons (1 oz, 30 g) butter or margarine

1 tablespoon freshly snipped chives

1 tablespoon freshly chopped thyme or marjoram

salt and pepper

2 tablespoons milk

6 oz (180 g) stilton cheese, crumbled or coarsely grated

Scrub the potatoes and prick all over. Cook in a hot oven (425°F, 220°C, Gas Mark 7) for 1 to 1 1/4 hours or until tender.

Cut the top off each potato and carefully scoop out most of the flesh. Mash the flesh and then beat in the butter, chives, thyme or marjoram, salt and pepper, and milk. Finally stir in 4 oz (25 g) of the cheese.

Spoon the potato filling back into the skins, piling it up as necessary. Stand on a baking sheet (oven tray) and sprinkle with the remaining cheese. Return to the oven for about 10 to 15 minutes or put under a moderate broiler (grill) for a few minutes until golden brown.

To microwave this dish, first place pricked potatoes on a paper towel in a microwave on HIGH for 6 minutes; turn and cook for 7 minutes. Fill potatoes as described above, then place in microwave on a paper towel as before and cook for 2 to 3 minutes more.

Serve with salads and garnish with fresh herbs. or use as an accompaniment to another dish.

Beef & Potato Mille-feuille

2 oz (60 g) low-fat polyunsaturated margarine

1 small onion, finely chopped

1 small head Florence fennel 4 oz (115 g), finely chopped

1 small dessert apple, about 4 oz (115 g), peeled, cored and finely chopped

2 oz (60 g) fresh white breadcrumbs

1 tablespoon each chopped dill and parsley

2 oz (60 g) salted cashew nuts, finely chopped

salt and ground black pepper

1 egg yolk

1 lb 6 oz (625 g) long, narrow piece roasting beef

1 tablespoon all-purpose (plain) flour

1 cup (8 fl oz, 250 ml) beef stock

sprigs of fresh dill to garnish

Potato Pancakes

1 onion, finely chopped

2–3 tablespoons sunflower oil

1 1/2 lb (750 g) floury potatoes, peeled

Melt half the margarine in a pan and cook onion, fennel and apple for 2–3 minutes until soft. Stir in breadcrumbs, dill, parsley, nuts, salt, pepper and egg yolk and stand to cool.

Preheat oven to 400°F (200°C, Gas Mark 6). Cut a deep pocket in beef. Shape fennel stuffing into a sausage, stuff into beef and secure with string. Spread meat with remaining margarine, place in a baking dish and cook in oven for about 1 hour.

Meanwhile, make potato pancakes. Cook onion in 1 tablespoon oil until soft. Grate potatoes, squeeze out excess moisture with paper towels. Add to onion with salt and pepper and mix well.

Heat oil in large frying pan. Drop 4 large tablespoons of potato into pan, flattening each into a neat round of about 4 inches (10 cm) in diameter. Cook for about 2 minutes each side until brown then make eight more in the same way. Keep warm.

Remove meat from baking dish and keep warm. Put dish onto stove, stir flour into meat juices and cook for 1 minute. Add stock and bring to a boil.

Remove string from meat, cut into 8 slices. Layer 2 slices of meat between 3 potato pancakes to form 4 'mille-feuille' stacks.

Strain sauce and divide among 4 warmed plates. Put a mille-feuille on each plate and garnish with sprigs of dill.

Cajun Roast Potatoes

SERVES 4

6 medium potatoes, cut into 2 inch (5 cm) chunks

¹/₄ cup (2 fl oz, 60 ml) vegetable oil

1 tablespoon Cajun Spice Mix (see below)

1¹/₂ teaspoons dried oregano or thyme

1¹/₂ teaspoons salt

¹/₂ teaspoon black pepper

Cajun Spice Mix

Makes about 1 cup (4 oz, 125 g)

¹/₂ cup (2 oz, 60 g) paprika

¹/₄ cup (1 oz, 30 g) black pepper

1¹/₂ tablespoons or more cayenne

2 tablespoons garlic powder

2 tablespoons onion powder

Preheat oven to 375°F (190°C, Gas 5). Place the potatoes in a large bowl and toss with the oil. Mix the seasonings in a small bowl and sprinkle over the potatoes. Toss to coat thoroughly.

Transfer the potatoes to a well-oiled baking dish and bake, stirring occasionally, for 45 minutes to 1 hour or until they are soft in the middle, crisp and brown on the outside. Serve at once.

These potatoes are delicious with roast or grilled meats and poultry. Leftover potatoes are especially good for brunch when fried briefly in a little oil.

Cajun Spice Mix

Combine the spices thoroughly and store in a closed jar in a cool, dry place. Add more cayenne if you want a hotter mix. Use within a month for maximum flavor.

Crab & Potato Casserole

6 small-medium potatoes

3 hard-cooked (boiled) eggs

dried dill

coarsely ground or cracked black pepper

1/2 lb (250 g) crab pieces or the flesh of two small fresh crabs

fresh-chopped chives

cheddar cheese for grating

2 heaped tablespoons flaked almonds

butter for browning

White Sauce

2 tablespoons (1 oz, 30 g) butter

1 clove fresh garlic, chopped

2 tablespoons all-purpose (plain) flour

1 1/4 cups milk

1 cup water

1 teaspoon salt

juice of 1 small lemon

Garnish

1 crab, cooked (optional)

Heat oven to 350°F (180°C, Gas Mark 4). Grease a baking dish with a little butter. Peel, wash and slice potatoes. Boil potatoes until tender. Drain and quickly arrange half of them on the bottom of the casserole so that it is completely covered.

Slice eggs thinly and arrange in a layer on top of the potatoes. Sprinkle lightly with dried dill. Grind black pepper on top. Make a layer of crab pieces. Sprinkle generously with fresh chives. Add a final layer of potatoes.

White Sauce

Melt the 2 tablespoons butter and sauté the garlic until softened. Stir in the flour and cook until pale yellow. Gradually stir in the milk and water; keep stirring until smooth and thick. Season to taste with salt. Remove from heat and add lemon juice.

Pour sauce over casserole, grate cheese over the top and then sprinkle with almonds. Sprinkle with fresh dill and dot with butter. Bake for about 30 minutes until golden brown.

Decorate with a whole crab for a dramatic touch.

Creole Potato Salad

8 medium, waxy-skinned potatoes, unpeeled

¼ cup (1 oz, 30 g) chopped red bell pepper (capsicum)

¼ cup (1 oz, 30 g) chopped green bell pepper (capsicum)

¼ cup (1 oz, 30 g) chopped celery

½ cup (2 oz, 60 g) chopped onion

1 teaspoon or more salt

½ teaspoon or more black pepper

1 cup (8 fl oz, 250 ml) Creole Vinaigrette

½ teaspoon or more Tabasco or other hot pepper sauce

½ cup (2 oz, 60 g) chopped scallions (spring onions) with green tops

¼ cup (½ oz, 15 g) chopped parsley

Cook the whole potatoes in boiling, salted water to cover until barely done, about 20–30 minutes depending on size. A sharp knife or skewer should meet some resistance when inserted. Do not overcook the potatoes; they are better a little underdone than overcooked. Cool until they can be handled but are still warm.

Cut the potatoes into ½ inch (1 cm) slices and place in a large bowl. Add the chopped peppers, celery and onion. Season with salt and pepper. While still warm, toss the mixture with the vinaigrette and Tabasco. Marinate for at least 1 hour at room temperature, turning occasionally. Before serving, toss with the scallions and parsley; add more salt, pepper and Tabasco to taste.

Creole Vinaigrette

Whisk together all ingredients except the oil in a small bowl. Gradually whisk in the oil. Creole Vinaigrette will keep up to a week in a covered jar at cool room temperature.

Creole Vinaigrette

Makes 1¼ cups (10 fl oz, 300 ml)

¼ cup (2 fl oz, 60 ml) red wine vinegar

1 tablespoon whole-grain mustard

2 garlic cloves, finely minced

1 teaspoon Cajun Spice Mix (page 10)

¼ teaspoon cayenne

¼ teaspoon Tabasco or other hot pepper sauce

1 teaspoon Worcestershire sauce

½ teaspoon or more salt

¼ teaspoon black pepper

¾ cup (6 fl oz, 175 ml) olive or vegetable oil

Filled Savory Potatoes

6 very large, oval, waxy potatoes, scrubbed but not peeled

choice of filling, about 2–3 tablespoons for each potato

Preheat oven to 400°F (200°C, Gas 6). Place potatoes directly on the oven rack and bake 1 hour. Insert a skewer into the middle. If it slides in easily and comes out coated in potato, they are ready. Remove and cool until they can be handled.

Alternatively, prick each potato all over with a fork, place on paper towel and microwave on HIGH until tender (about 5 minutes for 1 potato, 10 minutes for 4, depending on size and oven power).

Cut potatoes in half lengthwise and scoop out the middle, leaving about 1/4 inch (5 mm) inside to form a shell. Mix potato flesh in a bowl with choice of filling.

Scoop filling back into potato shell and top with any garnish. Place on baking sheet and return to oven 5–10 minutes to warm through, or reheat in microwave for 3 minutes.

Filling suggestions

- Drained, canned tuna mixed with a dash of sesame oil, dash of vinegar, a spoonful of grated ginger and some sesame seeds.

- Pesto with parmesan and ricotta.

- Chopped fresh dill, diced hard-cooked (boiled) eggs, cottage cheese.

- Chopped salami, fried with diced tomato and green pepper (capsicum).

- Sautéed onion, prepared mustard, and Worcestershire sauce.

- Sautéed sliced leek and bacon pieces.

- Sautéed onion and tomato with basil.

- Diced ham, cubes of cheddar or mozzarella, and dried or fresh oregano.

Frankfurt Potato Casserole

SERVES 4-6

6 medium-large potatoes, peeled

6 eggs

6 frankfurts

4 oz (125 g) ham pieces

3 cups seasoned cream sauce

butter

breadcrumbs

Seasoned Cream Sauce

2 oz (60 g) butter

2 oz (65 g) plain flour

1 pint (600 ml) milk

1 teaspoon sour cream

2 teaspoons Hot English mustard

1 tablespoon parsley, chopped

freshly ground white pepper

salt

Garnish

1 hard-cooked (boiled) egg, finely chopped

thin strips of red bell pepper (capsicum)

Hard-cook the six eggs. Boil the potatoes until tender. Prick frankfurts and simmer in water to cover, for 5 minutes.

Peel and slice the eggs. Cut the frankfurts into rounds and slice the potatoes. Arrange in layers in a large casserole dish. Sprinkle the ham over the top.

To make Seasoned Cream Sauce, melt the butter gently in a saucepan. Stir in the flour and cook until pale yellow. Gradually stir in the milk and increase heat to medium; keep stirring until mixture is smooth and starts to thicken. Gradually add other ingredients and simmer, stirring, until smooth.

Pour sauce over the casserole. Top with buttered breadcrumbs. Bake in a moderate oven, (350°F, 180°C, Gas Mark 4) for 30 minutes.

Garnish with chopped egg and red bell pepper strips and broil (grill) or bake for another 5 minutes or until the pepper starts to color.

Fried Potatoes with Chilies

2 lb (1 kg) red or white potatoes, unpeeled and cut into 1/4 inch (5 mm) dice

1/3 cup (2 1/2 fl oz, 80 ml) vegetable oil

1 medium onion, cut into 1/4 inch (5 mm) dice

1 poblano or 2 jalapeno chilies, stemmed and cut into very thin strips

salt

Heat the oil in a large heavy frying pan. Add the potatoes and stir to coat. Pat them into a flat layer and cook over medium heat for 10 minutes.

Stir in the onion and chili and pat into a flat layer again. Continue cooking until the potatoes are brown on the bottom, about 5 minutes.

Turn the potatoes, raise the heat to medium-high and cook until golden on the bottom, about 5 minutes more.

Transfer to paper towels to drain. Salt lightly and serve right away.

Lamb & Potato Moussaka

SERVES 4

3 large potatoes

1 lb (500 g) minced lamb

2 chopped onions

butter for frying

2 tablespoons tomato purée or paste

1/3 cup (2 1/2 fl oz, 85 ml) red wine

1 teaspoon cinnamon

salt and pepper

oil for frying

3 tomatoes

flour

breadcrumbs

extra butter

White Sauce

2 1/2 oz (75 g) butter

4 heaped teaspoons flour

1/2 pint (300 ml) milk

1 egg yolk

grated nutmeg

In a pan, fry the lamb and onions in butter until browned. Add the tomato purée or paste dissolved in the red wine. Add cinnamon, and salt and pepper to taste. Cover the pan and cook gently for 30–40 minutes. Sprinkle with chopped parsley.

Peel and finely slice the potatoes. Fry them in a pan, browning on both sides. Remove to a plate, select the three best-looking slices and keep them separate. Slice the tomatoes, reserve three slices. Flour the rest lightly and fry in oil. Lift onto greaseproof paper.

Butter a large casserole dish. Make a layer with one-third of the fried potatoes, to cover the bottom of the dish. Spread half the meat mixture on top and arrange on it a layer of tomato slices, then a layer of fried potatoes. Over them put the rest of the meat mixture, and the remaining tomato slices and potatoes.

To make the White Sauce, gently melt butter in a saucepan; mix in the flour, stir for one minute, then gradually add the milk, thinning with a little water if it becomes too thick. Simmer (do not boil) for 5 minutes. Remove from heat, stir in egg yolk thoroughly; add a pinch of nutmeg, then pour sauce over the potatoes.

Sprinkle with breadcrumbs, dot with butter and bake at 350°F (180°C, Gas Mark 4) for 30 minutes.

Just before serving, garnish with the reserved potato and tomato slices.

Latticed Mediterranean Salad

16 oz (500 g) cooked waxy potatoes, sliced

2 x 7 oz (220 g) cans tuna fish in oil

2 tablespoons lemon juice

freshly ground black pepper

4 large tomatoes, sliced

4 hard-cooked (boiled) eggs, sliced

2 oz (60 g) can anchovy fillets, drained

1/2 cup (2 oz, 60 g) black olives

Put the potatoes onto the bottom of a shallow dish.

Drain tuna, reserving 2 tablespoons oil and discarding the remainder. Flake the tuna and add to the potatoes.

Mix the tuna oil with the lemon juice and black pepper. Sprinkle over the tuna.

Arrange the tomato slices over the top of the tuna, then put a slice of egg on top of each tomato slice.

Cut the anchovies in half lengthwise, arrange in a lattice over the top of the eggs. Place the olives between the anchovy strips.

Serve at room temperature or lightly chilled.

Luscious Potato & Watercress Soup

SERVES 6

12 oz (350 g) potatoes, peeled and diced

2 oz (50 g) butter or margarine

8 scallions (shallots), trimmed and sliced

2 bunches watercress, trimmed and roughly chopped

3 cups (24 fl oz, 750 ml) chicken or vegetable stock

salt and freshly ground black pepper

¹/₂ teaspoon Worcestershire sauce

2 teaspoons lemon juice

1¹/₄ cups (10 fl oz, 300 ml) milk

6 tablespoons light (single) cream

6 tablespoons plain (natural) yogurt

watercress sprigs to garnish (optional)

Melt butter in a large saucepan and sauté scallions and potato gently for a few minutes without browning.

Add watercress to pan and toss. Add stock, seasonings, Worcestershire sauce and lemon juice and bring to a boil. Cover and simmer gently for about 30 minutes until tender.

Cool slightly and either sieve the soup, or purée in a blender or food processor, and return to a clean pan. Stir in milk and bring back to a boil for about 1 minute.

Thoroughly blend cream and yogurt, and add about half to the soup. Reheat gently and adjust seasonings.

Serve each portion with a spoonful of the remaining cream and yogurt mixture swirled through it, and you may like to garnish with watercress sprigs.

Mexican Potato Omelet

SERVES 6

4 medium unpeeled red or white potatoes, washed and cut into ¹/₈ in (3 mm) dice

¹/₄ cup (2 fl oz, 60 ml) oil

1 small onion, minced

2 jalapeno chilies, stemmed and minced

1 teaspoon chili seeds

salt

12 large eggs

warmed tortillas

Heat the oil in a large saucepan. Add the potatoes, onion, jalapenos and chili seeds and cook over medium-high heat, stirring from time to time, until the potatoes are soft but not disintegrating, 15 to 20 minutes. Sprinkle with salt to taste.

Meanwhile, break the eggs into a bowl and stir with a fork to mix the yolks into the whites.

Add the eggs to the skillet and stir to blend with the potato mixture. Cook over medium heat, gently pushing the setting edges into the middle without scrambling the eggs, until almost completely set, 10 to 15 minutes. Cover and continue cooking over low heat until firm, 3 to 5 minutes more.

Transfer to a platter without folding over. Serve right away with warm tortillas on the side.

Picnic Potato Salad *(illustrated inside front cover)*

SERVES 4

1 lb (500 g) small new potatoes

2 tablespoons olive oil

1 onion, finely chopped

4 oz (125 g) bacon, diced

2 oz (60 g) bell pepper (capsicum), chopped

parsley, chopped

Dressing

1/3 cup (3 fl oz, 90 ml) olive oil

2 tablespoons balsamic vinegar

1 teaspoon French mustard

1 tablespoon mayonnaise

Boil potatoes until tender, then drain. Depending on size, cut into halves, quarters, or leave whole. Set aside in bowl.

Heat oil and sauté the onion and bacon until bacon fat is transparent. Add to potatoes, then stir through the bell pepper and parsley.

Mix dressing ingredients together thoroughly and add to salad. Serve at room temperature.

Potato & Anchovy Pie *(illustrated opposite)*

SERVES 4

4 medium potatoes

2 small onions

2 oz (60 g) butter

2 tins flat anchovy fillets

2/3 cup (5 fl oz, 150 ml) cream

extra tablespoon butter

sprig of fresh dill

Peel potatoes, slice, and cut into very thin straws. Put in a saucepan with water to cover, and bring to a boil. Boil 1 minute, drain and rinse in cold water.

Slice onions and fry in half of the butter until transparent.

In a greased ovenproof dish, arrange layers, first of potatoes, then onions, then anchovies, then more potatoes, and so on.

Pour a little anchovy oil over the top, dot with butter and cook in a hot oven (400°F, 200°C, Gas Mark 4) for 45 minutes. Serve hot, garnished with fresh dill.

Potato & Ham Croquettes

SERVES 6

3 large boiled potatoes, mashed with no added ingredients

2 tablespoons butter

²/₃ cup (3 oz, 85 g) ground (minced) ham

1 ¹/₂ teaspoons flour

¹/₂ cup (4 fl oz, 125 ml) milk

1 tablespoon chopped parsley

salt and freshly ground pepper

dash of lemon juice

flour for dredging

2 eggs, beaten with a little water

breadcrumbs

oil for frying

Melt the butter in a pan, making sure it doesn't burn. Add the ham and heat gently for 2 minutes. Stir in the flour and then the milk, parsley, salt (omit if the ham is salty) and pepper; cook for 1 minute. Stir in the mashed potato and finally the lemon juice.

If the mixture is too dry, add a little more milk, but take care not to add too much liquid. Let the mixture cool, then chill in the refrigerator for at least 1 ¹/₂ hours and up to 2 days.

Form the croquettes in a cylindrical shape 3 inches (7.5 cm) long and 1 inch (2.5 cm) in diameter and dredge in flour. Dip into the beaten eggs, then coat with crumbs. For best results, chill the croquettes for at least 30 minutes.

Fry the croquettes in enough hot oil to cover, turning once. Drain on paper towels and serve immediately.

Potato & Mustard Seed Salad

1 lb (500 g) yellow-fleshed potatoes

1 tablespoon macadamia nut oil

1 leek, thinly sliced

2 cloves garlic, crushed

$1/2$ teaspoon yellow mustard seeds

$1/2$ teaspoon brown mustard seeds

$1/4$ teaspoon paprika

1 cup sliced snake beans

1 stalk celery, sliced

2 tablespoons ground, roasted macadamia nuts

Dressing

3 tablespoons mayonnaise

3 tablespoons soy drink (milk)

1 tablespoon macadamia oil

Choose yellow-fleshed potatoes for this salad and leave the skins on for additional dietary fiber.

Scrub potatoes, and boil with water to cover in a saucepan, or cook in a microwave oven, until tender.

Heat oil and gently fry leek with garlic, mustard seeds and paprika until leek is soft and seeds crackle.

Cut potatoes into $3/4$ inch (2 cm) cubes. Blanch snake beans in boiling water or in a microwave oven, place in cold water to retain a fresh appearance, then drain well.

To make dressing, mix all ingredients together, store in refrigerator until required.

Mix potatoes with snake beans, celery, mustard seed mixture and dressing. Place in a serving bowl and sprinkle with nuts. This salad tastes best when served at room temperature.

Potato & Parsnip Au Gratin

SERVES 4

1 1/2 lb (750 g) potatoes, peeled

1 1/2 lb (750 g) parsnips, peeled

salt and coarsely ground black pepper

1 onion, peeled and chopped

2 tablespoons (1 oz, 25 g) butter or margarine

3/4 cup (6 fl oz, 180 ml) vegetable stock

2 oz (60 g) edam or gouda cheese, grated

chopped cilantro (fresh coriander leaves) or parsley to garnish

Coarsely grate the parsnips, put into a saucepan, add a pinch of salt and cover with water. Bring to a boil for 2 minutes, then drain thoroughly.

Gently fry the onion in the melted butter until transparent. Add to the parsnips.

Coarsely grate the potatoes, mix with the parsnips together with the stock and plenty of seasonings.

Turn the vegetables into a well-greased heatproof dish (not too deep) and level the top. Cover with greased foil or a lid and cook in a fairly hot oven (400°F, 200°C, Gas Mark 6) for an hour.

Remove the foil and sprinkle with cheese. Return to the oven, uncovered, for 20 to 30 minutes until golden brown. Serve sprinkled with cilantro or parsley.

Potato & Pea Curry

1 1/2 lb (750 g) potatoes, peeled and cut into large chunks

2 tablespoons vegetable oil

2 cloves garlic, finely chopped

1 medium onion, finely chopped

2 teaspoons ginger, grated

2 teaspoons hot chili, minced (or hot chili paste such as sambal olek)

1/4 teaspoon cardamom seeds, cracked

1/2 teaspoon cumin

1 teaspoon turmeric

1/2 teaspoon garam masala

1 teaspoon salt

pepper to taste

1/4 teaspoon ground cinnamon

3 cloves

1 bay leaf

1 tablespoon lemon juice

2 cups steamed rice, to serve

1 cup frozen peas

4 tablespoons water

Boil potatoes in salted water to cover, for 10 minutes. Drain, rinse in cold water and set aside.

Heat oil in a large saucepan. Add garlic and onion and sauté until onion is soft. Add spices and lemon juice and fry gently for a few minutes.

Put rice on to cook.

Add potatoes, peas and water to onion mixture and mix well to combine. Cover tightly and cook 10 minutes.

Serve this curry with hot steamed rice and an Indian chutney or pickle. Of course, like all curries, it tastes even better the next day.

Variations

• Add 1 teaspoon mustard seeds after cooking onion and fry until they start to pop.

• Use less potato and instead add 5 oz (150 g) pumpkin, peeled and cut into large chunks. Add to boiling potatoes after 5 minutes.

• Before serving, sprinkle the curry with 4 tablespoons shredded coconut that has been lightly toasted under the broiler (grill).

Potato & Sprout Salad

1 lb (500 g) tiny new potatoes

8 scallions (spring onions), thinly sliced

1 cup (8 fl oz, 250 ml) light sour cream or mayonnaise

juice of 1/2 lemon

1 dill pickled cucumber, chopped

1 green apple, quartered, cored and chopped

freshly ground black pepper

flesh of 1 pomegranate

1 cup snow peas (mangetout)

1/2 cup mustard and cress or bean sprouts

3 tablespoons grated parmesan cheese, optional

Wash potatoes and cook, with skin on, in boiling salted water until tender.

Drain potatoes and mix with scallions, sour cream and lemon juice while still warm, to develop a good taste.

Leave to cool, then fold in dill pickled cucumber, apple and snow peas, and season to taste with pepper.

Cover and chill lightly. Thirty minutes before serving time, allow salad to come to room temperature.

Serve potato salad topped with pomegranate flesh, sprinkled with sprouts and cheese.

Potato & Zucchini Rosti

2 lb (1 kg) potatoes, peeled and coarsely grated

2 tablespoons vegetable oil

1 large onion, peeled and chopped

2 zucchini (courgettes) trimmed and coarsely grated

salt and pepper

1/2 teaspoon ground coriander

1 1/2 –2 oz (45-60 g) gouda or cheddar cheese, grated (optional)

Heat 1 tablespoon oil in a large pan, add the onions and gently fry until soft.

Put the grated potatoes into a bowl and mix in the zucchini and fried onions; season well with salt, pepper and coriander.

Heat the remaining oil in the pan and add the potato mixture. Cook gently, stirring occasionally, for about 5 minutes, then flatten down into a cake and cook until browned underneath and almost cooked through, about 6 to 8 minutes.

Sprinkle the top of the potato cake with grated cheese, if used, and put under a moderate broiler (grill) for about 5 minutes or until lightly browned.

Serve the potato rosti hot, cut into wedges.

Potato Galette with Chives

6 large baking potatoes (2¹/₂ lb, 1.25 kg)

3 oz (90 g) butter

3 onions, peeled and thinly sliced

2 oz (60 g) bacon rashers, derinded and chopped (optional)

salt and pepper

good pinch of ground nutmeg or mace

3–4 level tablespoons freshly chopped chives

Prick the potatoes all over and bake in a hot oven (425°F, 220°C, Gas Mark 7), for 1 to 1¹/₄ hours until soft. Cool slightly. Split the potatoes open and scoop out the flesh.

Melt 2 tablespoons (1 oz, 30 g) butter and very gently fry the onions and bacon (if used) until onions are transparent, about 10 minutes.

Mash the potato flesh adding seasonings, nutmeg, and half the chives.

Add the remaining butter to the onions in the pan and when melted add the mashed potato mixture. Stir thoroughly to combine, then flatten out to form a cake. Cook the potato cake on a gentle heat for 5 to 6 minutes until browned underneath.

Put the pan under a moderate broiler (grill) until browned on top. Carefully slide the galette onto a serving plate and sprinkle with the remaining chives. Serve hot, cut into wedges.

Potato Wedges with Aioli

6 large, waxy, white-fleshed potatoes, scrubbed clean

1 teaspoon salt

4 tablespoons all-purpose (plain) flour

1 teaspoon paprika

1/2 teaspoon cayenne pepper

2 tablespoons olive oil or melted butter

salt and freshly ground black pepper to serve

Aioli

2 cloves garlic, crushed

3/4 cup (6 fl oz, 180 ml) whole-egg mayonnaise

pinch of salt

lemon juice to taste

Place potatoes in boiling salted water and cook until just tender but not too soft, about 15–20 minutes. Drain, peel and slice each potato into quarters lengthwise to form wedges. Pat dry with a cloth.

Preheat oven to 400°F (200°C, Gas Mark 6).

Mix salt, flour, paprika, and cayenne pepper in a large bowl. Toss wedges first in oil or butter to coat, then in flour mixture.

Bake in a baking dish for approximately 20 minutes, turning after 10 minutes, until crispy and golden brown.

Serve sprinkled with salt and pepper, or topped with a little purchased salsa, and accompanied by aioli.

To make aioli, whip crushed garlic into mayonnaise. Add a pinch of salt and a generous squeeze of lemon juice to taste. Try adding sweet chili sauce or zest of lime for something different. Serve at room temperature.

Rich & Easy Potato Salad

SERVES 6-8

2 lb (1 kg) small new potatoes

2 sticks celery

4 scallions (spring onions, shallots) with some green tops

1 cup mayonnaise

1/2 cup (4 oz, 125 ml) sour cream

1 1/2 teaspoons Dijon mustard or horseradish cream

freshly ground black pepper

chopped fresh parsley, to serve

Vinaigrette Dressing

1 tablespoon white wine vinegar

6 tablespoons extra virgin olive oil

juice of 1 lemon

big pinch salt

Place potatoes in a saucepan of lightly salted water to cover, bring to boil, and cook 10–12 minutes, or until just tender. Do not overcook — they should be just tender when pierced with a skewer.

Drain and cool until easy to handle. Peel, if desired, cut into thick pieces and place warm potatoes in a bowl.

Mix dressing ingredients and drizzle over potatoes; toss lightly to coat. Cover and refrigerate 1–2 hours or until cold.

Trim and slice celery and scallions and add to potatoes. Combine mayonnaise, sour cream and mustard in a bowl. Season to taste with black pepper. Lightly fold mixture through potatoes.

Refrigerate until required. Serve well chilled, sprinkled with parsley.

Scalloped Potatoes with Bacon & Tarragon

SERVES 4

2 lb (1 kg) potatoes

salt and pepper

1 large onion, peeled and finely chopped

1 level tablespoon finely chopped tarragon or 1 level teaspoon dried tarragon

3 oz (75 g) bacon rashers, derinded and chopped

1 cup (8 fl oz, 250 ml) light (single) cream or milk

2 oz (50 g) mature cheddar or gruyere cheese, grated

fresh tarragon or parsley to garnish

Peel and dice the potatoes. Place half in a greased ovenproof casserole and season well. Sprinkle with the onion, tarragon and bacon, then cover with the rest of the potatoes, smoothing the top as level as possible.

Pour the cream over the potatoes and cover with a piece of greased foil. Cook in a hot oven (400°F, 200°C, Gas Mark 6) for 1 1/4 to 1 1/2 hours or until almost tender.

Remove the foil and sprinkle the potatoes with cheese. Return to the oven, uncovered, for 15 to 20 minutes until lightly browned.

Alternatively, place in a microwave and cover and cook on MAXIMUM (100%) for 10 to 12 minutes, then brown under broiler (griller).

Serve hot, garnished with fresh tarragon or parsley.

Smoked Cod & Potato Casserole

2 medium potatoes, peeled and thinly sliced

freshly ground black pepper to taste

1 tablespoon parsley, finely chopped

2 lb (1 kg) smoked cod

1 cup (8 fl oz, 250 ml) milk

1 egg, beaten

Place the potatoes in a saucepan with water to cover, and bring to a boil. Boil gently until just tender when pierced with a skewer. Do not overcook. Drain and rinse in cold water. Leave to cool until they are easy to handle.

Grease a casserole dish and lay most of the potato slices on the bottom. Season with black pepper and parsley.

Divide smoked cod into bite-size pieces and form into a top layer with the remaining potatoes.

Pour combined milk and egg mixture over the top.

Bake for about 25 minutes at 350°F (180°C, Gas Mark 4).

Serve with slices of lemon and a green salad.

Smoky Potato Bake

2 lb (1 kg) medium-large potatoes

2 tablespoons breadcrumbs

8 oz (250 g) smoked bacon

5¹/₂ oz (170 g) butter

1 lb (500 g) cottage cheese

salt

pepper

Boil potatoes until tender. When cool, peel and slice. Sprinkle a deep, well-greased oven-proof dish with some of the breadcrumbs. Place a layer of potato over this.

Chop bacon and fry until crisp. Scatter half the bacon over the potato in the dish. Melt the butter and cheese in a saucepan over a low heat. Pour half of this over bacon and potatoes. Add another layer of potatoes and another layer of bacon. Pour over the remaining butter and cheese. Season to taste. Sprinkle the rest of the breadcrumbs on top and dot with butter.

Bake in a moderate oven, uncovered, for 30 minutes. Cut into generous slices and serve.

Spicy Sausage & Potato Casserole

SERVES 8

2 lb (1 kg) potatoes

12 oz (375 g) haricot beans

4¹/₂ pints (2.8 litres) hot water

12 oz (375 g) moist (tender) prunes

4¹/₂ oz (145 g) Csabai or other hot, smoked sausage or salami

sugar

salt

Put haricot beans into a saucepan with about two-thirds of the water (enough to cover well). Bring to the boil for 2 minutes, skimming if necessary. Remove beans from heat. Leave to stand in water for 1 hour.

Meanwhile, soak the prunes in the rest of the water and peel and dice the potatoes.

Drain the beans, then bring to a boil in fresh water. Add diced Csabai and potatoes when the water is just beginning to boil, then turn down heat to a simmer. Add prunes, salt and sugar to taste when beans are nearly tender.

This dish is ready when the potatoes are very tender. Total cooking time is about 2 hours.

Spinach & Potato Circle

Base

1/2 lb (500 g) packaged frozen spinach

2 oz (60 g) butter

2 onions, finely chopped

2 tablespoons all-purpose (plain) flour

I cup (8 fl oz, 250 ml) milk

1/2 teaspoon nutmeg

salt and pepper

4 oz (125 g) cheddar cheese, grated

Topping

2 lb (1 kg) potatoes

I oz (30 g) butter

1/4 cup sour cream

I egg, lightly beaten

4 chopped scallions (spring onions)

3 tablespoons chopped parsley

2 tablespoons chopped chives

salt and pepper

Garnish

I hard-cooked (boiled) egg, quartered

Base

Cook spinach according to packet instructions and drain well. Sauté chopped onion in butter in pan until tender. Stir in flour until golden brown, gradually add milk, stirring until sauce boils and thickens.

Add the spinach and nutmeg, and salt and pepper to taste, and cook for a further 3 minutes. Put the spinach in a casserole dish, reserving a heaped tablespoonful.

Topping

Cook peeled potatoes in boiling salted water until tender, drain well. Mash the potatoes, add butter, sour cream and egg, and beat until smooth. Add scallions, herbs, salt and pepper to taste, and mix well.

Place an upturned glass in the middle of the spinach in the casserole dish and spread the mashed potatoes evenly around it. Sprinkle with cheese. Remove glass. Bake uncovered in a moderate oven (350°F, 180°C, Gas Mark 4) for 20–25 minutes or until golden brown.

Gently heat the reserved spinach and use it to form a fresh circle of spinach where the glass has left an opening. Garnish with egg quarters and serve.

Warm Potato Salad

1 1/2 lb (750 g) small new potatoes

salt and pepper

6 tablespoons salad oil

1 tablespoon wine vinegar

grated rind of 1/2 lemon

1 tablespoon lemon juice

1/2 teaspoon Dijon mustard

1 teaspoon superfine (caster) sugar

2 oz (60 g) can anchovy fillets, drained and finely chopped

2 tablespoons capers

4 scallions (spring onions), trimmed and chopped

1 tablespoon freshly chopped parsley

12 black olives

Scrub the potatoes but do not scrape or peel. Cook in boiling salted water until just tender. Alternatively, place the potatoes in a covered bowl with 4 tablespoons water in a microwave on HIGH for 9 to 10 minutes, then let stand for 8 to 10 minutes.

Make the dressing by beating together the oil, vinegar, lemon rind and juice, seasonings, mustard, and sugar until emulsified. Mix in the chopped anchovies, capers, scallions, and half the parsley.

Drain the potatoes and cut any large ones into pieces so they are all the same size. Add the dressing to the hot potatoes, toss thoroughly and quickly turn into a serving dish.

Add the black olives and sprinkle with the remaining parsley before serving.

Potato Varieties

Every country has its own range of potatoes available in the marketplace at different times of the year, and potato names differ in each region. New varieties are also constantly being created by growers. As a guide, some varieties are shown in the photograph opposite, and listed below. Many of those shown will be very similar to varieties in your own region which have approximately the same type of flesh, and therefore similar uses. Check the varieties shown to see which potatoes are best suited to the range of cooking techniques and dishes with which you are familiar in your own kitchen.

Bintje
Oval shape, pale yellow skin, creamy yellow flesh. Use for deep-fried chips, boiling, mashing, sautéing, salads, gratins.

Coliban
Round shape, white skin, white flesh. Use for jacket-baking, boiling, mashing.

Desiree
Long, oval shape, smooth, pink skin, yellow flesh. Use for boiling, mashing, jacket-baking, roasting, salads.

Kipfler
Small, long, knobbly shape, yellow skin, yellow flesh. Use for salads, jacket-baking, roasting, mashing.

Kumara
Kumara is the New Zealand Maori name for a purple-skinned vegetable with golden flesh, also known as Sweet Potato. The Australian vegetable (shown here) has orange skin and orange flesh. Use for mashing, purées, roasting, deep-fried chips.

Nicola
Medium, oval shape, cream skin, yellow flesh. Boiling, mashing, salads.

Pink Eye
Round shape, creamskin with pink eyes, yellow flesh. Use for boiling, mashing, jacket-baking, roasting, salads.

Pink Fir Apple
Medium, long, knobbly shape, pink skin, yellow flesh. Use for salads, boiling, jacket-baking.

Pontiac
Medium-large, round shape, red skin with red eyes, white flesh. Use for boiling, mashing, salads, jacket-baking, roasting.

Russet Burbank
Medium-large, oval shape, rough white skin, white flesh. Use for deep-fried chips, jacket-baking, roasting.

Sebago
Medium, oval shape, white skin, white flesh. Use for mashing, salads, jacket-baking, roasting.

Sweet Potato
Despite its common name, this root vegetable is not botanically related to the potato species. Large, long irregular shape, white skin, white flesh. Use for mashing, purées, roasting, deep-fried chips.

Other Varieties

Atlantic
Round shape, rough white skin, white flesh. Use for deep-fried chips.

Bison
Round shape, red-purple skin, white flesh. Use for boiling, mashing, jacket-baking, roasting.

Kennebec
Oval shape, white skin, white flesh. Use for deep-fried chips, mashing, jacket-baking, roasting.

King Edward
Small, oval shape, pinky-white skin, white flesh. Use for boiling, mashing, roasting, deep-fried chips.

New Potatoes/Chats
These are usually small potatoes of the Coliban or Sebago, or similar, varieties. Small, round or oval shape, white skin, white flesh. Use for boiling, salads.

Patrones
Medium, oval shape, cream skin, yellow flesh. Use for salads, boiling, mashing, jacket-baking, roasting, sautéing, gratins.

Red la Soda
Large, round shape, red skin, white flesh. Use for boiling, mashing, salad, jacket-baking, roasting.

Published by Lansdowne Publishing Pty Ltd
Level 1, The Argyle Centre, 18 Argyle Street, Sydney 2000, Australia

Chief Executive & Publisher: Jane Curry • Creative Director: Sally Stokes
Publishing Manager: Cheryl Hingley • Editor: Nicholas Szentkuti

Designed by Kathie Baxter Smith • Front cover photograph by Andrew Elton
Printed in China

ISBN 1 86302 534 0

IMPORTED BY/IMPORTE PAR
DS-MAX CANADA
RICHMOND HILL, ONTARIO
L4B 1H7

ENGLAND
PRO-SALES DIRECT LTD
278A ABBEYDALE ROAD
WEMBLEY
MIDDLESEX HA0 1TW
ENGLAND

MALAYSIA
PRO ENTERPRISE SDN BHD
LOT 605, SS13/1K, OFF JLN.
KEWAJIPAN, 47500 SUBANG JAYA
SELANGOR D.E., MALAYSIA

DS-MAX
FOOTHILL RANCH, CA 92610-2619
IMPORTER: #16-1241510
949-587-9207